Joyful Spirit

Angela Mitchell

To, Kelly.

Love,

Angela Mitchell

2024

Messages inspired by Spirit

Contents

This book is dedicated to my brother Bobby Rao, who passed away on March 12, 2023, a week before his 59th birthday. I hope you are flying free wherever you are, Bobby.

Acknowledgments:

My family in Spirit: My parents – Maria and Patrick Rao, my grandmother, Ammai, and my mother-in-law, Pauline, continue to inspire and support me in my work as a Medium.

This book would not be possible without the wisdom of my Spirit Guides, Yellow Bear, and the Guru. I am humbled and grateful to channel your words and philosophy. Most of all, I thank my husband, Peter, for believing in me and giving me the courage to be who I am meant to be. I also wish to thank my sister Jackie for supporting my work. I want to thank from the heart so many people, including Mediums and audiences at Spiritual Churches, Church committees, tutors, and my dearest friends, who listened and encouraged me.

Foreword

In February 2024, I was very ill and ended up in hospital. While drifting in and out of consciousness, I saw faces, colours, and swirls of energy around me. I also felt very supported and loved. I was in a deep sleep and fought desperately as something told me *I wouldn't wake up if I did.* The faces became clearer, and I saw my mother and my guide, Yellow Bear, beside her. I heard both of them say, "You have to wake up! "You have so much work to do." My mother gave me a book; my name was on the cover. Their voice, still in my mind, said it was a book they would give me from the Spirit world, and it would be used to inspire people. As soon as I was well again, I started writing this book and found pieces I had written over the years channeled by my guides.

I hope, my dear reader, that the words of Spirit will uplift and inspire you.

Angela Mitchell

July 2024

Berkshire, UK

"It is not in doing what you like, but in liking what you do, that is the secret of happiness."

— *J.M. Barrie, Peter Pan*

A Balance of Time

If we view every day as a gift from a higher power, we will appreciate life much more. There is no guarantee that we will wake up each time we lay our tired heads on the pillow for sleep. Most of us know of someone who did not see another sunrise or sunset, leaving us vulnerable and questioning life and death.

Never take life for granted. While we should not live like there is no tomorrow, we should also be reminded that tomorrow is not certain.

What is the solution then, my friends? Well, live a **balance of time** so that you don't put off things that you can do today to the future. Do what you can now and free the future for new projects and experiences. Don't clog up the future with a long to-do list that makes it harder to manage and clear. Those in Spirit wish they had not left so much unfinished as they have seen how loved stress themselves out sorting matters on their behalf.

Don't wait for the right moment to do certain things in life. The right moment could be right now. However, we have to release ourselves from this careless approach to time to see it. If we have such a loose opinion of time, we genuinely do not appreciate every moment, second, month, or year. Taking time for granted makes us a little lazy and maybe even cheat ourselves of achievements, enjoyment, and experiences that could enrich our lives in the present.

Don't put off calling someone or visiting a sick relative when your intuition tells you to because of work or a busy lifestyle.

You cannot buy back time. The sun always rises, but it also sets. It is up to the higher power for which it sets and rises.

Nature's Gift to Humanity

The most significant gift from God is most definitely nature. We have so much to be grateful for from the air we breathe, the winds, the sea, plants, and flowers. From the humble potato to the microgreens in a Michelin-star restaurant, nature provides for all regardless of age, sex, race, or financial status. What we perceive as exclusive or of a higher grade is entirely man-made.

Unlike man, Nature does not judge or discriminate. The roses in the garden grow beautifully despite knowing that they will eventually be cut and placed inside the home, bringing cheer to the household. Such is nature's selflessness. It does not expect anything in return and has always existed to feed, nourish, and be there for humanity to enjoy.

Like the many things we take for granted in life, nature deserves our love and respect. Sometimes, just acknowledging the miracle of nature itself is a gesture that will also make you feel good and connected to the unseen energies around you.

Nature is life and nourishment for the soul. How often have we felt genuine connection and love at seeing a bird, especially a robin? Or walking in the woods amongst ancient trees that have seen so much more of life than you have as they stood the test of time? When did you last hug a tree or hold a flower to your chest to feel pure love?

Use Nature to feel the stillness and authentic connection to our higher selves. This is a free and uncompromising relationship that we can enjoy at any time without any judgment. Do this often to discover peace within and an appreciation for life that money cannot buy.

Spiritual Purpose

Many of us will seek a more spiritual purpose at some point. Even if this is 10 seconds before we transition or at a tender age, it will happen in one way or the other. The hardest of hearts can change and soften to search for meaning when the time is right. What this means to one person will be different to the next. While the common perception of "spiritual" and "purpose" is meditation, spirituality, yoga, or healing, it can be having a change of heart, moving from a self to a selfless nature.

No one has a right to dictate someone's spiritual purpose or path. It is up to the individual to journey step by step and then come to that realisation on their own. When the "aha" moment happens, the individual has a choice — to acknowledge, accept, and transform or to leave it as it is. There is no right or wrong way.

If the individual feels there is a better way of living or experiencing life but chooses to keep going, then it is their right to do so. For those who want to alter certain aspects of their lifestyle or situation, the search begins unless presented to them at the same time as the awareness.

For example, if someone feels very stressed and unable to cope with life, they may receive a breakthrough from the Universe. This could be anything from a solution to a problem or becoming aware they need to breathe better and find ways to calm their minds. Spirit may send someone their way in the form of a meditation or art teacher. The classes could help the individual find a new perspective on life and eventually find other pathways to live a less stressful life.

Spiritual purpose is not the same for everyone. Some will go on a journey to serve others, such as working as a medium, psychic, wellness teacher, or writer on spiritual topics. For others, their purpose will be to find a spiritual way of living.

So keep an open mind about your spiritual path, and do not compare yours with others. You are an individual with different needs and mindsets than others. Life has too much competition and comparison, so let your purpose be yours alone when making decisions.

Traces of You

Land, status, and material gain are all temporary earthly markers of success and power. Somewhere in the world lays the body of someone you used to be in another life.

The house you live in now will belong to someone else in 80 years. Your precious diamond ring will sit in a drawer for years or be sold by your loved ones. All that will remain of you will be a memory and a feeling, so start building your legacy now.

Your shadow and voice will disappear, but your actions will stay with people; therefore, make sure it is something people can draw inspiration from.

Lay your foundation with love, kindness, good deeds, and words so that people will remember how you made them feel. Start by being compassionate, kind, and respectful to yourself and extend that to others.

How you feel is vital, as it can affect how you make others feel. Starting with yourself and including others becomes easy and natural. Traces of you will slowly evaporate with time, just like water in the sun, but your actions, legacy, and love will live on forever in the minds and hearts of those you have touched throughout your life.

Show the World Who You Are

The Spirit World sees many of us struggle with how we present ourselves to the world. From body image to confidence to feeling different from everyone else. They ask us to accept ourselves for who we are and be brave as we show the world that we are different, acceptable, and enough. There is no need to hide ourselves or our talents. What we don't understand when we are in this mind space is that there will be five who will for everyone who doesn't believe in us. It is up to us to find that five people.

Please don't limit yourself or live in the darkness because of fear; it does nothing except create destructive patterns in our lives until we acknowledge it. The very thing you deny yourself maybe your life purpose; therefore, it cannot be shut away forever.

The Spirit world sometimes sees you agonise and feel isolated in your thoughts. What you perceive as a weakness may well be your biggest strength.

So don't be afraid to show the world who you are and live life without regrets.

I Am Right Here

Why do we have to die for people to think about us? So many of us feel so lonely and isolated with no texts, phone calls, or messages from people to ask, "Are you okay?

Why do we have to die for people to bring us flowers? Why can't we surprise a friend or relative with some flowers when they are alive?

Why do we wait for occasions? Why can't it be "just because? We do not have any use for flowers when we are gone, but receiving flowers can cheer up a grieving heart, put a smile on a tired soul, or brighten someone's kitchen on a cold morning.

Why do we sit and talk to our loved ones when they are gone but find it so hard to do so when they are alive? How many of us have whispered to a loved one in Spirit, "I wish we could have talked more? Why do we let our egos stand in our way of saying sorry or letting go of things when we are alive?

To live a good life without the "why," do the things you can do now rather than after someone dies.

Make living joyful and meaningful. Don't wait for people to die to miss them.

Spirit on Pain

Why do you experience so much pain? Mankind questions this throughout life. Whether the pain is of abuse, trauma, mental or physical, these challenges are often life-changing, crushing, and difficult to deal with. Not everyone deals with it in the same way. Imagine there is a big hole hidden by some leaves on a path. One person stumbles on it and falls into the hole but manages to crawl out as quickly as he falls. There is dirt on his trousers and a little tear, but he keeps going. The following person who falls in hits her head as she falls and waits for someone to help her. Meanwhile, another senses there is danger ahead and turns around. Everyone handles challenges differently, as there is no one perfect solution. You are individuals with minds, feelings, and limitations that are personal to you. It would be best not to compare yourself to others who can cope more easily.

You have these situations because through pain comes creativity, understanding, and insight. Sometimes, you are given these painful situations that feel raw and make you feel vulnerable, angry, and uncomfortable. In your human journey, dark times are necessary to find answers and your life purpose at the end of the experience. Embrace the moment and quieten down. Your answers are within, but you sit in pain to seek them.

Spirit on their Human body

I speak collectively and plainly for us in Spirit. We have no attachment to our physical bodies. It is removed once we have left it. It was merely a vessel for us, nothing more.

Please remember, my friends, that we are only attached to and attracted by your love for us. Our bodies may crumble and take themselves back into nature; however, our love and care for you continue.

We are energy and continue to vibrate and radiate as a collective, no longer as individuals.

Do not forget us as we have not forgotten us.

Stunning

When time began in the Universe, everything was motionless and silent. The quiet was part of the progress and creativity. We cannot create or build in chaos.

Love was the motive and beauty – the purpose. Love was both the intention and the tool.

The quiet you experience now is preparation for the deep tranquillity you will enjoy when in Spirit.

The sound of each and everything you take for granted now on earth will be 100 times more potent in our world.

The ringing of the church bells will vibrate longer and fill your entire being with each note. The slight sound

of a leaf falling to the ground, which you take for granted now, is deafening in my world.

Do not be disheartened if your sound is small and unheard now because we hear you.

Enjoy the hush now and then, for it allows you to think and appreciate the tranquillity within.

In our world, we are energy and sound. The simplicity allows us to see and be seen.

Silence is stunning.

Be still. Be silent. Be stunning.

A Prayer for Life

Dear God, Divine Spirit, and those in the Angelic realm who shine their love upon us. Thank you to our Spirit family, friends, and guides for providing comfort and wisdom to our lives. Thank you so much for another day.

Thank you for the breath that allows our hearts to beat, the food that nourishes our bodies, all the material things that make our existence more comfortable, and most of all, the family and friends who make our lives worth living.

Divine God, please wrap your energy around every one of us so that we can feel your healing power and love. Please teach us to forgive quickly and let go of the pain, resentment, and anger that cloud our lives.

Please bring gentleness to our nature, strength to our bodies, and power to our souls.

Divine Spirit help us forgive easily, forget our wrongs, and concentrate on our rights.

Let us live a lighter, loving, and positive life. Let us be love.

Amen

Your Guiding Light

Speak, for they will listen. Seek for they will come

Rejoice because there is a celebration.

Expand for there is space.

Fear not, God, the Divine is with you.

Do not deny what is within you

Be in your power and be who you are meant to be

You can do whatever your mind is determined to do. Do not let self-doubt and others sway you.

Be productive and get things done. Be open and accurate, but also be yourself.

Please don't compare yourself to others who may be comparing themselves to someone else.

All this means is that you judge yourself too harshly and bring pain to your soul.

Pour light and love into yourself so that instead of pain, there is only self-love and freedom of expression.

Speak your truth and inspire others with your honesty

Be proud of who you are because that is who you are meant to be

Your guiding light will shine brighter when you understand that the future can be bright.

When we focus on the dark, that is the only thing we will see, not the little flame in the distance waiting to light our path.

So, always move towards the light whenever darkness creeps into your mind.

I am in Your Heart

Do not put flowers on my grave or shower my headstone with your tears,

I am not there, my love. Why would I be there?

I am with you as you make my favourite dish or around the table when you speak of me.

I am by your side when you go to sleep with tears on your pillow. I send you healing as we grieve together.

I miss you too, my love, but I am never far from your mind.

I am in that thought, the memory and the pain.

I laugh and cry with you, so don't talk to my ashes, my love, for I am not there, nor am I in the grave.

I am the bird that sings to you on a cold winter morning

The gust of wind on a hot summer day or the soft voice in your head that you dismiss as your imagination

I am the little star in the sky that blinks when you say my name. I am with you in the stillness of the mind when you wake up. The breath you take as you drift to sleep

I am the thousand sighs you take, the light in the corner of your eye, and every beat of your heart

For I am one with you, my love. I am your heart.

Be Curious

As we grow older and the burdens of life weigh us down, the little things get forgotten, like being curious. Remember when, as children, we never feared things, always asked questions, and were inquisitive about everything and everyone? As adults, we self-impose conditions on our behaviour, thoughts, and actions that can stop us from being curious, spontaneous, and accessible. There is an excellent reason to be childlike. It frees our souls to explore our potential as humans and remove limitations.

So many of us adults struggle with personal freedom, fear new experiences, and constantly struggle with the fear of failure. These can all be crippling to some and can stop us from truly enjoying life. Those in Spirit, who now benefit from hindsight, can see how much those on the Earth plane, self sabotage their happiness.

Be enthusiastic about life, your purpose, and your path. You cannot find what you don't search for. If you want to find meaning in life, be open, question everything, and never stop wanting to learn more. Remember the child within you whenever everything feels difficult. You will see life as an opportunity to learn and thrive without restrictions.

Learn to live Without Your Loved One.

It is natural to feel life is not worth living or that you cannot go on when you lose someone important. Some people leave a massive void in our lives, which is both painful and so crushing that we cannot see beyond the grief and how we feel at that moment.

How will a birthday feel without a mother's home-baked cake or granddad's bad jokes at the Christmas table? Whom will you share your worries about work or, worse still, who will walk you down the aisle?

Even though the soul thrives after death, its physical body and presence are gone, and this is what we humans miss the most.

We have got to know the physical presence of our loved ones, not their souls; therefore, we miss what we know.

The challenge for many of us is to continue to live when our loved ones pass away.

Living with the dead means we continue our journey without our loved ones who have passed, learn to laugh, thrive, and make every moment count. We can also learn from their mistakes, forgive, and heal our pain.

What we don't want to do is shut down our own lives, stay in a negative state of mind after a loss, and let a part of us die with the dead.

Some become a shadow of themselves after a loss and struggle with life. Our family and friends, in Spirit, do not want us to stop living.

They do not want us to die with them. They want us to continue to live, flourish, and make the most of life.

So, learn to live without your loved ones.

Learning to Let Go

Sometimes, the easiest things to do are the hardest. Letting go is one of them. At some point in our lives, many of us have been told to "let go" of people, situations, and even material things. If it were that simple, then none of us would have an emotional attachment to the past. We subconsciously hold on energy from an argument, a breakdown in friendships, an acrimonious divorce, being talked down to by a parent or even at school, being bullied, and so much more. People will remember how you made them feel; sadly, many of us remember the negative feelings, not the good ones. If we focus on the nice things people have said, lovely gestures, or words of wisdom by a grandparent, our thoughts will centre on the feeling. We can use this vibration to motivate and inspire us daily. What we pay attention to impacts our energetic field and multiplies. So, if yours is only on the bad, you will see a pattern emerge, duplicating a similar memory or pain but manifesting itself differently than what you may have experienced. For example, if you had a parent who told you to "keep quiet" when you tried to speak as a child, and as an adult, you feel that that made you feel small and what you had to say was not important, then similar situations at work or with bosses at work will recur until this is healed. The sooner we can view certain situations in the past as the past and focus on the other good things, the less difficult our future and present will be. Many of us have not one but several things that hold us back in this way.

It is Okay to Cry

Have you ever noticed how nature looks brighter, the air feels fresher and even the colors of the plants look brighter after it rains? This is nature's way of clearing the energy.

While crying is commonly perceived as bad or sad, it can also be a cleansing ritual to help us release pent-up emotions and help us see things better. Humans are very good at keeping things within and not expressing ourselves. Sometimes, this dates back to childhood, or perhaps it is in our personality to not burden others with our worries or problems. Whatever the case, it can be overwhelming to hold on to things for too long, and if the urge to cry becomes strong, don't suppress it. Let the tears flow, and give yourself the space to acknowledge your feelings.

Crying is not a weakness and is not limited to women or children. Allow yourself to cry regardless of gender or age. Sometimes, we need that release to feel better, lighter, and hopefully calmer. Clarity comes when we can step back and see things from a calmer state of mind.

So, give yourself the freedom to cry. It is a natural thing to do, and we don't need to feel sad to cry.

It is okay to cry.

Ambition

Make your way of life simple and truthful so your path is clear. There is no harm in having big dreams and ambitions that may feel too much to other people, but if that is your desire and path, then it is yours alone to fulfill. Do not stray from your morals and ethics to achieve them, as the path will lead to a bleak and unfulfilled space.

Keep your heart pure and your mind clear to create the right mindset for achieving your goals. The Divine rewards those willing to dream big but work hard to attain them honestly.

There is no need to diminish others' light to make yours brighter. There is enough light and love for everyone in this world. Sometimes, shining someone else's light can also brighten yours. Supporting others on your way to success will create a positive chain of people who will lend a hand when you need it.

So be ambitious, but don't let your ego take over to make you become someone you never meant to be.

Reminder to Self

I don't have to do what everyone else is doing

I don't need to be someone to be something

I don't need to be ashamed that I am different

I shouldn't have to change myself to fit in with the crowd - for I am unique, and I am perfect as I am

Yes, I would like to work on some things, but that doesn't mean I need to change who I am.

I am free to change with time and through lessons learned in life

This is all part of evolving into who I am meant to be

I can be unlike others yet be part of the same collective. Like a puzzle, it takes a lot of different pieces to make a full picture. I have a lot to contribute as I am.

I have talents, knowledge, and experience that can help others and accept help from others for what I lack or don't yet have

I am who I am, but I also give myself the space to grow so my energy is always dynamic and open to progress.

I will not stifle my development by trying to emulate others or feel I am not enough.

As a reminder to myself, I am enough, and I am someone.

Worries

Humans are conditioned, from a young age, to worry. We spend so much time worrying about the small things that we risk losing focus on the bigger and more important things in life. How many of us look back now and realise that we worried about things that didn't matter? Worrying takes energy and depletes us. It is also a very negative state of mind. Has anyone felt refreshed and positive while fretting about something? The answer is no. You are likely to feel stressed, anxious, and overwhelmed with fear. It is important to understand what you can control, which means you can change the situation and things you have no control over. This way, you can transform your thoughts to be more positive. Understanding what you can't control means you know you can do nothing to control the situation; therefore, what is the point of worrying? If we spend more time distinguishing between what we can and cannot control, we can reduce worrying and inaction, which sometimes is part of that process and creates destructive patterns in our lives.

This is not to say that you shouldn't worry about certain things, but spending most of your time worrying about everything can be draining. Focusing on what we can change and taking the necessary actions will enable us to lead a more productive and happier life, which is ultimately what we all strive for.

Being Kind Even When in Pain

One of the hardest things to do when you are in pain, whether physical or mental - is to be happy for someone else who is celebrating a happy moment or success.

When we are wrapped in our agony, there is no light, spare emotion, or thought to give to anyone else. We are within this energy that envelopes our very being. It can sometimes feel like a very negative, upsetting, and angry space. So when people share their happiness, be it a material success, a marriage, or having a new baby, It will feel like a light shined on your failures, flaws, unhappiness, or even grief. There will be times when you may feel like, "How dare they show off their happiness when I am going through so much pain? Many people in this age of social media do not think of anyone else. They may genuinely want to share their happiness with everyone and have no intention of showing off or upsetting anyone. However, for the person suspended in the bubble of hurt, everything will feel aimed at them.

The truth is, the birds will continue singing, the trees will continue to grow, children will be born, and wars will still be fought in the world regardless of what happens to each of us. How we deal with our pain and suffering while others thrive is up to us. We can be kind and not be offended or upset by everything.

You can celebrate their success and be supportive without being unkind. You do not need to compare their success to your situation. Use any learning lessons from their achievement to help your progress.

If you are grieving and cannot feel any form of joy because you lost someone so important in your life you cannot see beyond the pain, then please allow yourself the time to heal.

Do not lash out at others because you are wounded. Rather than resenting people's happiness, see it as a light to show you the way out of the darkness of grief. There will be a time when you will be happy again and slowly heal that pain.

In the meantime, be kind to others and be patient because your moment will come.

Miracles

We are often told to expect miracles when we pray; however, most of us cannot help but feel disappointed when things don't happen immediately. The divine's timeline is very different from ours. What we want may not be what we need right now. We could want something to happen, but the sequence of things required to take place before could take longer; therefore, it is not so simple for even the divine to conjure up a miracle. Our wants are often related to the material, whereas the Divine is more concerned with the progress of our soul, life purpose, and happiness. The wonders and magic will manifest when both our intentions align.

We miss the fact that waking up every day is a huge miracle. There is no guarantee we will wake up when we go to sleep each night. Having a child is a miracle, and for those who were able to get an organ transplant, a second chance at life is a gift that money cannot buy.

Always express gratitude for what you have and ask for miracles that are not always material. You will see a positive change in your life that will last a lifetime rather than the short-term satisfaction of objects.

You can ask the Divine for help, but be patient; it will manifest when the time is right.

Inner Beauty

Your inner beauty is as unique and pure as a newborn baby. It is unrelated to your looks or how you present yourself to the world. Your inner beauty is more important than how beautiful or well-dressed you are to others. Your inner beauty is your SOUL and your LIGHT within. Many of us spend much time on our outward beauty yet pay little attention to what is within us. The inner pureness is vital to our progress and is what the Divine sees and values. They do not care for how our hair or shoes look. Our souls endeavour constantly for the quiet so they can speak their truth to us for inspiration and alignment. If we spend more time nurturing from within, there will be no lack of confidence or feeling inferior to others. We will not see people for the physical façade they put on; we see their souls to see their true beauty. Nurture yourself through meditation, sitting in the quiet, walking in nature, and truly connecting with the Divine to bring peace and harmony into your live

Use your inner light to inspire and love others. You can also use it to light up your life through self-love, appreciation, and acceptance. You will find that uplifting others will be effortless, and your ability to move on from difficult situations will be much quicker and easier. When your Soul is shining bright, so will your outer beauty.

A New Day

Each day, we open our eyes, take in the smells of the room and the home, feel the sheets around us, and see the sunlight streaming through the windows, which is another day to experience life. We must take it one day at a time and not let problems, decisions, and arguments make us feel that each day is a burden. Always remind yourself at the start of each day that it is a new opportunity to look at things differently. The anger could be soothed in the hours you were asleep, and a problem could be solved. However, you must be open to these things; otherwise, everything will build within you until it consumes you. Accept what you cannot change and change what you cannot accept. A new day is a chance to make amends, change your direction, and even question your decisions. A new day is a new chance to make new memories with people you love, make decisions that can transform your life, and experience a short time in your earthly life.

A new day is a new space you can paint with all the colours of life, so what you choose to do with it is yours. You can make it positive, memorable, or frustrating and burdensome—the choice is yours.

The new day is a state of mind, so let go of bitterness, anger, regret, and jealousy. Focus on yourself and how to make the most of life and the moment.

A new day is an opportunity, not a burden.

Spiritual Development

Spiritual development should be viewed as a way of developing one's natural ability for connection. It starts and ends with you. It should never be used as education for a purpose. There is no end or beginning with development. You will never stop learning, and it will never be enough. Once you open your eyes to what is in the invisible world, you will never stop wanting to absorb and stretch your mind. Development is not a race, and it should never be a competition. In our fast-paced world, many want instant results in development and then get frustrated when it doesn't unfold as naturally or as easily for others. Development is a very personal and complex journey for each individual. Some people may have reached a certain stage on their own, consciously or subconsciously, to enhance their knowledge, while others may be at the very beginning and need more help. Expansion of your energy and mind needs constant practice and dedication. Many expect to be fully ready to work as a medium after a workshop or course without having done any self-reflection or understanding their SOUL and energy. There is no rush or finish line to reach. Stop, slow down, and appreciate every moment so you truly understand your journey and mediumship before you can even attempt to teach others.

Instead of being frustrated by the lack of progress, stop and examine why it has slowed down. Are your intentions aligned with your purpose?

Do you feel pressured to reach a milestone, or have you been putting what you have learned into action? Questioning yourself this way will help you progress.

Mother and Child

Unconditional love is something that most Mothers give to their children, regardless of how old they get. The link between a mother and child is irreplaceable. However, one does not have to have blood links or have given birth to that child to have this connection. An adoptive mother will love her child as fiercely as a biological mother. Motherhood is not limited to just children who have touched the earth plane. The love between a stillborn in Spirit and an earthly-bound mother is eternal, and they will miss each other until they are reunited one day. Sometimes fear, outside influences, health, or surroundings prevent some from having a good relationship with their children or mothers. Even if no love is shown during a lifetime, love is everlasting, pure, and free from judgment in the Spirit world. Not everyone experiences a healthy relationship with their mother or children. There will be those who have a break down in communication, leading to arguments or even falling out.

One may be speaking from experience or a deep hurt, and the other, of the future and trying to break down a wall of defense. Don't give up and let the facades prevent you from your future. Do not let your differences move you away from your similarities. Listen to understand, not judge, respond, or dismiss. Let each other be heard and understood. Because when it is too late, your word will remain stuck in your mind and unsaid. All you will have is memories and echoes from the past. So say what you need and want to say when you are both here. It is never too late to apologise, and never too early to say I love you.

Being Uncomfortable to be Comfortable

There is a circle within life that we often miss because it is so momentary. The moments that take you out of your comfort zone and make you feel uneasy, followed by a positive experience or outcome, are vital to our growth. It teaches us that expansion is not possible without space to grow. Staying in a state of mind or situation without movement cannot bring about change or total transformation, no matter how hard we want it. When we encounter such points in time, it will feel unpleasant and scary, so we resist it as much as possible. Usually, these leaps of faith will be followed by a pleasant outcome that could be life-changing, bring about immense happiness, or help you grow.

The more we recognise and embrace these junctures, the easier life will become. We can take greater steps forward if we reduce the time spent resisting change or something new.

Often seen as painful, challenging, and difficult, these moments are gifts within our human experience. It helps us grow and become who we are meant to be, not hinder us.

This is LIFE, so embrace every moment, even if it's difficult because it wants to take you somewhere right for you.

Don't Cry for Me

Don't cry for me, dear one

For when the day starts and ends without me

And your eyes are filled with tears

I am unable to wipe them away, for I have no hands

I wish you wouldn't cry.

I know you want my physical presence, not my Spirit, for you don't know me that way. I watch as you are unable to stop the tears from falling. The wall of pain stops you from seeing me each time you think of me, my dear

I am there to see each time the sun rises and the soft rays touch your hair. Each day is a gift for you, my dear, not a burden on your way to being reunited with me

So when each day begins and ends without me,

Keep me in your heart, but let your mind be free to live and enjoy the moments. There will be no regrets when I receive you on that special day.

We can watch the sunrise and sit with each other when we are reunited, my dear

Keep me in your heart, my dear one

I have never left your side and am always there with you. So don't cry now, my love

The Spirit World

We are not in a different world from yours, my friend

We are not in a dimension or space

We are not far from you, and your thoughts

Why do you distance yourself from us?

Do you not want us to come close?

We are as near as your breath and the air you breathe in

Because you can't see our physical body, you dismiss us, but our energy holds our thoughts, memories, and intelligence

Until your consciousness is expanded and clear to perceive us, we will always feel far from you

Mediums have only a small window into how things are with us

Your awareness is only limited by your ability to see beyond the physical

Take People As They Are

We often feel disappointed in people when they don't meet certain expectations we have of them. It is natural to feel let down when they don't return our loyalty, love, or honesty. We look for values or characteristics in people that match our own.

The truth is that some people can't give you what they don't have for themselves. How can they be loyal to you when they betray themselves by self-sabotaging their lives?

Those who are fighting with their demons cannot give you love because they have yet to find a way to love themselves. How someone who lies to themselves be truthful to others? Don't expect others to give you what you need. Take people for what they are, not what you want them to be, for they will disappoint

We will be less disillusioned by people if we truly understand who they are and what they can offer as they are.

Mediumship

Mediumship must come from the heart and should always be of service to the Divine, not as a vehicle to feed the ego. It is not a performance nor a way to elevate oneself for fame and glory. A medium's place on a platform is not a given right but an honour and privilege to serve. A Medium's role and purpose is to provide comfort, healing, empowerment, and closure to the living and those in Spirit. It is not for those to use Mediumship falsely or for financial gain. There is nothing wrong with being rewarded for serving Spirit; however, there is a difference between working in a heart space and only being interested in the rewards.

Those not in service to Spirit will eventually find that while success may come quickly, so will disillusionment and disconnection. Do not blame Spirit or the Divine or call it "a spiritual crisis" when this happens.

Interruption in progress occurs when a Medium is not aligned with the Divine. It is a chance to correct one's purpose and intention to see if the path chosen is valid or has deviated from the course. Use your Mediumship wisely and always work from the heart to sustain yourself without losing sight of your purpose

Fly Free, Little Bird

Fly free, little bird, for you are no longer in pain

Your broken legs are now replaced by wings that will take you far and wide. The body that served you well is no longer, but your shell is not needed in our world

You are no longer limited or burdened by your physical body, for in Spirit, all we have is energy, memories, and intelligence. There are no restrictions in our world, just freedom and expansion

Fly free, little bird, as you are now released

All that worried you every day and night is no longer

Come to us and take flight; our world welcomes you with the brightest lights and love. As the sun sets on the end of your physical life, a new dawn awaits you in Spirit. A chance to finally be truly loved unconditionally, to remember who you are, and to explore and grow beyond what you have known

Fly free, little bird, and come towards us as you leave all that you have known for so long behind

Don't worry, my love, you will still be with them, but the time has come for you to come home

Fly free, little bird with us, for we await you with the purest of love.

Fly, little bird, you are now free

Small Boat in the Middle of the Sea

Sometimes, life may feel like being on a small boat in the middle of the sea without an oar or direction.

The sea is choppy, impulsive, and unforgiving

The wind, unkind and gentle all at once

The silence is broken up occasionally by the sound of the fish as they push against the current to keep up with the school. The journey is both thrilling at times and unbearable. In the midst of this, you have an opportunity to understand why you are adrift and decide on your destination. Once you understand where you went wrong, you can correct your direction and find your way.

When you finally get to the shore and your body is rested, the hardship before slowly fades away. Another trip will begin, perhaps not as grim. Now and then, we go on these expeditions without a purpose and endure situations that feel unfair and unbearable. Over time, with enough reflection and self-awareness, we learn to determine our destination before setting off sail. Our ability to navigate choppy waters is negated by our ability to check on ourselves and the direction so that we correct mistakes quickly.

So, if you are on a little boat floating around in the sea without a purpose, stop, think, and understand why you are on the boat, where you want to go, and what led you to that point. Learn from your mistakes and recognise your flaws. Sometimes, we need to be more logical than emotional, as the heart and mind have different motivations. Following the heart in certain situations is not always useful, and the mind can be too logical in some. Knowing which one to pay attention to for guidance can greatly help.

Just remember, a small boat in the middle of the sea can reach its destination like a big ship.

Memories

No one can stop us from leaving our bodies when it's time. There is only one earthly experience in one body with one soul. There is one life to live, experience, and then leave behind.

All the material things we spend all our lives accumulating will be discarded or used by someone else. They will never hold the same meaning as they did to you.

The only truly important things you can take to Spirit are memories made with family and friends.

People who love you would prefer your time and love instead of gifts or material things.

Value your time with people and spend it wisely so that when your time comes, you will all share these moments eternally.

These memories and moments will continue when you are all in Spirit.

A Mothers Love

I fell deeply in love from the moment I knew you were there. I felt you even though you were the size of a peanut. I lay there at night, wondering if you were warm enough or too warm inside me. I felt you move before they said you would. I dreamt of your face each night and your hands around my belly.

We were one, not two, for I know you were mine, and I was yours. I spoke to you in my mind and heard your voice in my heart. I wondered what you would look like and whether you would sound like me or your dad.

I hope you'd have my lips and his eyes but not his nose

But his ears are perfect, while mine is odd

Regardless of how you turn out, my love for you will be eternal. For you are a part of me, my beautiful child

I know I will struggle when you are difficult, and you will hate me when I say no. But as we grow old together, you will see why I sometimes couldn't say yes.

For you see, my mother's love for you is everlasting.

Knock on the Door

Stop if you try something that doesn't work, but keep going without success. You cannot go through a locked door without a key, so if you can't get into the next room without help, this is not for you. Something should never be so rigid and unforgiving when it is meant for you. Your doors may be resistant at first, but they should open after a bit of patience. Don't waste your time battering down doors that will never open for you.

Success depends on how soon you realise what is working and what is not. Understanding this saves you time and energy, as spending too much time being frustrated only results in negative thoughts that do not serve your needs.

There are times when you can move boulders to build your dreams and other times when you can circle them to find another path forward.

So don't knock on locked doors to find your dreams. There may be another way; you have to find it.

For my Father

We never saw eye to eye most of the time, but it didn't matter as I think you read my mind most of the time.

You knew what I wanted before I asked and sometimes understood more than you showed. I knew I shocked you with my thoughts and actions because they differed from yours.

All you saw was a child you wanted to protect and love. I am no longer a child, but in your eyes, I have not grown from that baby you held in your arms.

So yes, we didn't agree on many things, dear father, because we never listened to understand, only to defend. I had the energy of youth and you, the experience of the old. Somewhere, somehow, we managed to find a balance. You were firm yet kind, angry but very gentle, and tired sometimes, but you always had time for a chat. Your words and insight into life make sense now that I am older and you are no longer.

I wish you could see that I listened, my dear father.

I miss your voice and your words of wisdom.

Lose to Gain

Sometimes, in our lives, we have to lose something to gain something. This could be letting go of a limiting emotion or situation or perhaps one you subconsciously impose on yourself. When you release fear, you find freedom and courage to take a leap of faith.

Letting go of fear helps you to try again when things fail. Releasing a betrayal opens the path to new and meaningful relationships without always comparing them to the past. You will start believing in yourself when you stop doubting yourself and build confidence. Show your authentic self to the world by letting go of masks and self-importance because that is not who you truly are. Let go of the past to walk into the future enthusiastically and with hope. Letting go or losing is not always negative. It can release you from the shackles that hold you back emotionally, mentally, and spiritually.

A Medium's Journey

A Medium's path is long and often complicated, but it will lead to a place of love and, ultimately, of service. If you concentrate on this intention, the trials and tribulations presented to you on the way will be nothing more than minor inconveniences sprinkled with life lessons. While it is natural to want praise and appreciation, please remember that it truly belongs to Spirit.

Being of service to the Divine and Spirit is all the acclaim you need as Mediums. Do not lose sight of the WHY when on the platform where your words and actions can and will influence the sitters and Mediumship. Mediums are part of the beautiful communication triangle that allows the unseen world to be acknowledged. It is a divine path that brings humanity closer to remembering their true purpose on earth and understanding a whole other world within their own.

Those who feel they are a celebrity or star or only do this work for monetary rewards are not aligned with Spirit. They will have lessons to learn, be brought down to earth, feel unsure about themselves, and find their way back to the divine. This is not to say that mediums should not be successful because Spirit does not want them to suffer and struggle financially.

There is a balance to be struck, and as long as one is aligned and humble, one will be compensated in all the right ways. When it is less about Spirit and more about the

Medium, then the purpose and alignment are apparent for all to see. Remember, you cannot fool yourself or us in the Spirit world. Your Spirit and those in the Spirit world are all-knowing and united in promoting love, healing, and the joyous reunion of our two worlds.

The Purpose of the Past

Do not be a prisoner of your past, for it will not serve your future. Your earlier years are not meant to be a life sentence for your mind to dwell on and not be able to live your life. The past is not your future, and your future is not your past. Take the lessons from previous years and evolve to better yourself for the future.

Challenges and pitfalls in front of you will be missed, causing failure, frustration, and distress. History will repeat itself repeatedly until you can learn from it and break the cycle. These trials can be easily maneuvered with the knowledge gained and recognised before it occurs. So don't confine yourself to old experiences and situations that limit your present and future life. Find a way to heal and look forward, no matter how difficult or traumatic the experience is, as there is a reason why you survived and managed to get to where you are now.

Yellow Bear's Message to Mediums

Mediumship is not a race. Focus on the journey, not the destination. If you get stuck where you want to be, you will be trapped in your old ways and not flexible. Your destination will change along the way. Your needs and wants will be different, and your path, if you are adaptable, will be full of learning lessons that could enhance your journey.

Do not feel that you need to compete or emulate someone else who you feel is more successful or has a bigger presence than you. Trying to be that person will not make you a better medium or more successful. Remember that each individual is unique in personality, ability, confidence, speech, and energy. You can duplicate words and style, but you cannot be that person.

Your mediumship will flourish if you focus on your development and spend time within yourself. Your inner connection is more important than anything else; the external noise you invite into the mind will limit it. Learn to be flexible, as Mediumship is an evolving infinite energy. Allow your journey to be dynamic, energetic, and unpredictable, as that will take you closer to the divine than a fixed plan.

Easter Message – Light After Darkness

The true meaning of Easter is there is life after death, and there is light after a dark time. For many Christians, Good Friday is a dark day of sacrifice and pain when Jesus died on the Cross. Those of us who have experienced loss will resonate with the white-searing pain that cuts through our hearts almost immediately when someone dies. The inconsolable moments when the world lost its meaning and life is unbearable. For many, Good Friday is a day full of grief and pain mixed with the sadness of a higher being so selfless for mankind, but it also reminds us of our grief.

Like the initial agony, we learn to live and smile again. For some time, the smile masks the excruciating numbness and ache. Slowly, we start to find the strength to keep going, to do mundane tasks without tears, and somehow, we smile and mean it.

The Reunion of Mankind

A soul's journey begins once it has moved away from the physical body, not the end, as most of us are led to believe. The body we take on and grow into is a vessel for our life's journey on Earth. However, once we discarnate, the body is shed, but the soul remains and moves back into Spirit. This is where the reunion takes place with not only the soul's earth plane family and friends but also those from previous lives and the soul group. This reunion is of pure love, void of judgment, and timeless. Imagine the friends you have whom you don't speak to often, but the moment you meet, it's like no time has passed; that is precisely what this reunification is like. For those left behind, with memories, pain, and regrets, the grief is a huge loss that sometimes takes even a lifetime to get over. Some will carry this burden until the day they are reunited. The Spirit world wants more of us to understand the importance of this REUNION because once someone passes, we can rejoice and mourn for them. While the pain of losing someone can feel like the heart is ripped out of us, the knowledge that they are in safe hands and will be met by all those in Spirit who will love them unconditionally could be a source of comfort. The Soul's journey does not end after death; it continues, keeping its memories but creating new ones, either in Spirit or as a new life on Earth.

Please hold this in your hearts—for everyone you lose; there is a reunion waiting when it's your time. Be excited to have this wonderful gathering on a different plane, with much knowledge and love far beyond what you experienced on Earth.

Flower, not Seed

Every day, I stood in fear of everything I held dear

Opportunities passed me by while I stood still and was afraid to fly

I felt stuck and hard done by life, yet it was my own doing that let my dreams die

One day, I realised that I was stopping myself from moving, not anyone else. Nothing was preventing me from doing anything.

It was me, saying "I can't" that was the challenge

But when I started saying I can, I saw the change

The more I said yes, the challenges turned into opportunities. I was able to embrace my capabilities instead of focusing on my weaknesses.

I looked at my strengths and offerings

Then I realised my value and my power

Don't limit yourself to a No. Allow yourself to flower because you are not meant to stay as a seed.

There will be Light within Grief

It takes time, but there is a glimmer of happiness after the initial pain of loss. Do believe that someday, the tears will be replaced by smiles, memories of those silly moments, and photographs of happy times.

You will remember the late-night conversations when your eyes were closing with sleep, but you both didn't want the night to end or the birthday cakes that flopped.

All these moments will flood in and replace the painful images imprinted in the mind when a loved one dies.

It will take time, but you will see the light in your time of darkness, for there was so much to rejoice about. The life lived, the laughs shared, and the emotions expressed. Do remember the bad times, like the silly arguments and the rash decisions that changed the relationship, but don't dwell too much on the fact that it brings up regrets and sadness.

The good and bad are part of human design: to live, experience, and move on to spirit. The only way to heal is not to dismiss but to acknowledge and let go, for there is light in the darkness. It takes time, but you will get there when you are ready.

Anger

Anger and to be angry is a negative emotion; however, it is also very much a part of humanity as is, laughter. No one chooses to be angry. Sometimes, it is their inability to express themselves adequately, frustration, feeling insecure, their situation, such as the feeling of helplessness, or simply that there are people around who make them angry. These are only a tiny example of why anger rises above laughter and happiness in people. Everyone, even those we look up to as peacemakers, would have lost their temper and been upset at some point because we are humans with many emotions and responses. However, we must be aware of how we affect others and how long we stay in that negative space. If our anger hurts or upsets others to the point of harm, then we need to stop and evaluate our behaviour. Whatever the reasons for anger, there is no reason for lashing out at others. They likely want to help and support you, but anger clouds clear thinking. Therefore, well-meaning words and actions will feel like judgment. If people themselves trigger you to be angry and lose control, then look to have more positive and encouraging people around you. The company we keep can influence our behaviour – both good and bad. The other thing to consider is whether it is okay to be angry, but how long? Some people can go through their entire lives being angry, forgetting what made them angry.

Life with anger is one of unfulfilled dreams and limitations, not just for the individual but also for their families. Anger limits you from feeling and being your best, so be angry if you need to be, but heal, let go, and move on. This is the only way you can bring light into the darkness.

Nothing is Permanent

Whatever concerns us today will be replaced by something else—a worry, a pleasant experience, or a solution. Nothing is permanent.

Today is one day in the days of your life. Don't let one day rule your week, month, year, or life.

There will be bad days, but there will also be plenty of good days. Remember and appreciate the good days because falling into the darkness stops us from reaching for the light.

Start every new day with a fresh heart and mind, creating a positive intention. If things don't go as you want, brush yourself up and keep going.

Don't let ONE day dictate your life.

Travel for the Soul

When you travel to see the world, you are opening your eyes and soul to new experiences and joy that bring clarity to your life. Seeing how others live or express themselves offers a different perspective that could enhance our lives. As humans, you are not meant to stand still and be in only one place. You are meant to move, see, listen, and experience life fully. Travel can be both enlightening and enjoyable. It doesn't have to be one or the other. A luxury holiday can be as joyous as backpacking with very little money. One could give you the relaxation you need while the other, adventure. A journey can open our minds and hearts to new people and thoughts to bring home. No travel is wasted, even ones that do not go to plan.

Lessons can be learned and implemented.

Travel is a natural part of humanity. After all, we have journeyed from the Spirit world to enter the physical world and grow within our mothers' wombs. You are meant to experience life and see more than your home, city, or country. This is why the Divine made the planet diverse from nature, people, cultures, languages, and food. During a journey, long or short, there will be things to discover that are missing from your life. The trip could very well change your life and enrich your soul. The truth is that the soul strives for diversity and growth, which travel offers in abundance. So listen to your intuition, as it is the compass that will guide you to your next destination.

How long will I love you?

As long as the stars shine bright on a clear night

Till the harvest moon illuminates the sky

Until my heart beats and in every breath, I will love you like there is no beginning or end.

I loved you even more when you didn't feel your best, like when you wanted to hide from the world because your hairline was thinning or a dress didn't fit.

My heart was full when you smiled so widely; your eyes lit up brighter than a Christmas tree.

Your laugh sounded like a beautiful windchime on a summer day, even though you thought it was too loud.

How long will I love you? I cannot say when it will end, as my love is eternal. I will love you even if we are no longer together, and I cannot see your smile.

Because you are in my heart and deep inside my soul

How long will I love you?

Forever and ever.

The Difficulty of Living

The difficulty of living is that I have to go on without you. Each day when you were here was a reason to carry on. Every night was made better by the fact you were near. The day you left was when everything I held dear was lost forever. Here I am, lost and defeated, without you.

The difficulty of living is the emptiness I feel

Memories flood my senses when I think of you

The sinking feeling follows as I remember I have lost you

Even a clear blue sky looks dull to me now. A rainy day felt sunny when you were here. How do I carry on without your love?

I am learning to find a way out of this pain.

The last breath and the way you looked before you passed are still etched in my mind. In time, I hope your beautiful smile and how you looked before will be what I see when I think of you. Your voice and how you felt on a happy day will always stay with me.

I hope to keep living without your physical presence, knowing you are always with me in Spirit.

I know the voice I hear in my mind when I ask for help or speak to you is you.

Until the day we reunite, it won't be easy to live without you, but somehow, I will make the most of it. So when we finally see each other again, I will have stories and a life to share.

Do not Seek External Validation.

You have the power

You are special

You are important

You are the change

You are the person who can make YOU complete

You are enough as you are

Please do not give your power away to others by thinking they will complete you. No one can make you happy if you can't be satisfied. They cannot give you what you don't already have. People can add to your happiness as you can to theirs, but no one has the power to provide it to another person. Heal yourself before you try to heal others or expect them to do the same for you.

You can love without asking and be happy without external validation.

Credentials

The only credentials you need to work with Spirit is love. No certifications or diplomas will make you a better spiritualist if you have no love to give. Love pours out without discriminating against race, nationality, status, or even beauty when your heart is open and pure.

Sleep Now, Dear Brother

My dear brother, the time has come for you to sleep and rest. For you, life was but a blur—rushing here and there, always on the go. You never walked on the grass, sat under a tree, or did something for fun.

Your time was never yours; time was the only thing you needed. I remember when we were children, and I would always find ways to wake you up.

My jokes and stunts sometimes make you laugh and, at other times, irritate you. Even as a teenager, all you wanted was to rest. Perhaps you knew that adult life would be complex and full of responsibilities.

Your physical body was heavy with life's burdens and full of pain. Worry and fears of the future weighed down your mind. When the call came that day, my heart was shattered, dear brother.

We never spoke about that argument, and I didn't get to ask you how you were. I know now that you were desperate to share your worries and needed comfort.

Sleep now, dear brother, for you have eternity to rest and recuperate. I wish I could wake you up as I did when I was young, but I know we will meet again.

So rest now, dear brother, for we will have much to do when we are together.

You are now free to do all that you wish you could have done and go to places far beyond your imagination. Sleep now, dear brother, for I will be with you one day.

Until then, shine your light from your world so I can see my path. Until that day, dear brother, let me always feel you around me. Sleep now until we meet again.

The Progress of Mankind

You are all unique and individual on the Earth Plane. No two people have the same mind, personality, or even physicality. Even in twins, there will be something to distinguish between the two individuals.

When the world was created, the Divine and the collective decided to make two groups – male and female. They were given unique personalities, looks, skills, and minds. While all humans come to the Earth plane and grow from seed to babies, they develop their uniqueness after age four or five. Before it enters the embryo, each soul decides on its pathway and understands how and when it will end. Once the baby is born into your world, the soul's memory is suppressed, allowing the child to discover its path naturally and organically without intervention.

The intention of the Divine was for humans to celebrate their differences. However, free will has resulted in the opposite. Those on the Earth plane have subjected each other to pain, suffering, comparison, and hate because of their differences. A decision was made to add more genders. This is why more and more genders are rising daily to push the boundaries until they are all blurred. The great Divine has learned that something needs to change through humanity's progress. While mankind has made incredible progress in many areas, discrimination within the human race has never moved forward.

So many thoughts were shared from different levels of consciousness in our world: Should there have been only two genders created and only one skin colour? Or would Men have discriminated over eye and hair colour?

There was an agreement to try adding more genders and encouraging interracial marriages to create a more harmonious race. Hopefully, this will eventually change how humans behave towards each other, focusing more on similarities rather than differences in the future. This is a true testament to growth and learning even within the Divine.

What was put into place at the beginning is not working, so changes are being slowly implemented to shift mindsets.

There is still a way for this progress to be made as humanity resists the changes.

We encourage you to be part of the transformation; do not wait for others to start the revolution. Do yours in a small and meaningful way. Open your hearts and minds to unity.

Beauty is Love

The Divine created Mankind to be imperfect. What you may perceive as perfection is what you can see and admire on the outside. Beauty, in the eyes of the Divine, is not perfection. In our world, beauty is when an individual has overcome human constraints to be filled with love.

You are beautiful if you are love in intention, action, and thought. When you start to appreciate your perceived imperfections, then the journey to accepting and loving yourself begins.

When you can accept and love yourself, your entire being, including your energy, is filled with love. This enables you to see life positively, which will result in happiness. In the Spirit world, we have no physical body and no beauty standards to achieve. The pureness attracts us within each soul's energy and capacity to love.

Man's purpose on the Earth plane is to let go of the need to be perfect and to seek perfection in others. You must also see beauty within rather than being obsessed with what you see on the outside. Learn to celebrate yourself and see past the exterior. The more mankind can get to the stage where inner beauty.

You are Strong

You are not strong because you held back the tears

You are not strong for keeping your grief quiet

You are not strong for smiling through your pain

You are strong because you are walking without me

Keeping me in my heart even though it's broken

Walking on with legs not strong enough to hold you up

You are strong, my love, for all that you do

Remembering my laughter as well as my last breath

Keep going, for you have so much to do

My physical life has ended, but never doubt that I am
with you. For we walk together, you see

I am with you every step of the way

For I never left

So be strong my love.

We are together forever.

Our memories entwined until the day of our reunion

You are strong with every sunset

Every morning, you wake up

Every breath you take without me

We are together, so be strong

The Brotherhood of Man

The great Divine encourages authenticity in mankind. When one's words and actions are aligned with one's heart and soul, there is nothing to fear or be guilty about.

Your words will be true, and your actions need not be scrutinised. Beware that you will be found out when your words and actions are unreliable. It may take days or even years, but the truth will be clear.

The compassionate Divine will allow you to go as far as possible on your journey as your false self. There will be many opportunities to turn around, make amends, and learn from mistakes.

Eventually, if behaviour or actions are modified, harsher learning lessons will be placed in your life. This does not mean that the great Divine believes in punishment; however, if your soul's journey was meant to transform while living this life, it will face a crossroads of change.

Your path on the Earth plane is to grow and learn from mistakes. Some will never be learned until the time of transition.

Come Back

As I sat in your favourite chair, tears filled my eyes. I can still smell your scent on the fabric. I desperately want your warmth to embrace me and soothe my pain.

Please come back to me; I don't care what or how. Just come back so I don't have to miss you so much.

Be the butterfly that sits on my hand when I think of you. Or the bird that sits on the fence when I drink tea in the garden. Please come back to me, my dear one.

I will be waiting for you. Be the smile of the newborn baby that reminds me of you. I will smile back and hold you, dear.

Please come back in some form. I miss you.

Empty Pockets

Many times in our lives, we feel that we simply do not have anything to give to anyone.

Yet we do not value what we have—compassion, a listening ear, or even a kind word that could make a difference to someone in need. When people are struggling, they do not need flashy cars, expensive presents, or nice restaurants.

A compassionate heart that truly listens without judgment and a warm hug can do more for someone in pain, grieving, tired, and hopeless.

When we start focusing on kindness and the emotional aspect of our humanity, the material starts to lose its power over us.

Most of man's problems are caused by money and material things. Your pockets may be full, but there is no happiness or peace if you do not have compassion or love in your heart.

An empty pocket with a full heart will find its way to happiness and peace

Remember when you feel you have nothing to give, you have so much more than your empty pocket.

Open your heart and let your kindness fill your pockets.

You are richer than you feel you are, and your empty pockets are full for the right people.

People on your Path

Everyone you meet in life has something to contribute to your growth. Some will enlighten you and help light up the path. Others will cloud your thoughts and heart with doubt, pain, and anger. You may even come across those who teach you to be kinder or push you to realise who you are. Imagine that every one of us has a big invisible blueprint that describes our path, life purpose, and even personality. Things that we don't know about ourselves but little by little, as each day, month, or year is unveiled to us. Now consider this - every single person you encounter has a pen that joins the dot on this blueprint which makes it visible to you.

Very slowly as the dots become clear, you see the truth about yourself, why things are the way they are, and where you need to go.

It is human nature to celebrate the good and dismiss the bad. Not everything that seems bad or difficult is what it is. Sometimes good is disguised as bad as part of the lesson. If everything just came easily then mankind will never learn or grow on the earth plane. Each time a person who poses a challenge appears on your path, use it to learn from the experience, about yourself and your purpose. Some will teach you that not responding to someone's anger is a solution while others may help you reach your full potential.

Someone who appears to be highly critical of you and delivers the truth in its rawest form will initially hurt and destroy you. Do not question why they said it, but understand what was said. What can you learn from this to improve and do better? Your biggest critics can spur you further than your best cheerleader.

Be Joyful

In life, hardship will come and go, be joyful anyway

When people hurt you or twist your words, stay calm

Believe that you CAN get up and go on when you fall and think you can't get up. When your happiness is at its lowest and you feel empty, be happy anyway

If you can't see the future, look for it. Be joyful anyway my dear one. Joy multiplies and changes your energy. If something bad happens and we sit in that space, we achieve nothing but more misery. When you focus on joy, it helps you see the way forward and moves you out of that dark space. In life, we have many choices because of free will So why not choose a positive emotion that clears the path?

Be joyful anyway

The Message in Hardship

When something feels hard, you have two options. One is to push harder to get past a particular stage. The other is to reevaluate and understand why there is so much resistance. In the first option, your hard work and determination will see you get through challenges and find success - in some cases, it is worth the effort but needs more action. Meanwhile, when you are on the wrong path, or trying to do something that is not right for you, or it's not the right time, or perhaps needs tweaking - it will be DIFFICULT to do. So, taking a moment to reflect will give you the clarity required to make things right.

Sometimes, we can be like a bull in a China shop— rushing into things without thinking or noticing the red flags. This is where the Universe shows us what is working and what is not.

You are Nature

You are nature. You are not one with nature or a nature lover. You are nature. You are part of the entire creation, which is nature. There is no difference between you and trees, ants, or birds in the forest or the park

You all have a purpose, a soul, a life, a journey, and a reason to exist. You may think you are far superior to the animals in the forest because you have a home with modern comforts, heating, and food.

Animals, however, look at humans, chained to technology, choked with worries, and locked in fear as prisoners in their own homes.

Animals in nature have endless freedom and a natural survival instinct and are not bound by where they live. Many of them know when to leave and when to stay. They know their purpose clearly, even if it is to be prey.

Just remember, dear ones, that just because you have nice shoes on and the deer runs without one doesn't mean you can run further than the deer.

So remember, dear ones, that you are nature, so appreciate yourself as well as every little flower, blade of grass, or butterfly you encounter on a walk.

Give thanks for being part of this earthly experience, as it will never be repeated. This is a once-in-a-lifetime chance to live in this body and with this soul.

Sit with Spirit

There will be times in your life when you feel overwhelmed, unappreciated, unloved, and alone. Although you may be surrounded by many in this physical world who would come forward to support you, you may not have the words to reach out and ask for help.

When these feelings come, they multiply and evolve, so much so that it will be hard to remember where it all started. Was it grief? The loss of a job or relationship? The cutting words uttered by someone you love?

In this moment of desperation, there is no beginning or end. Many will suffer silently and spiral into an unbearable darkness. The Spirit World encourages each one of you to remember that you are simply not alone, and your worries do not fall on deaf ears. You are heard loud and clear. Your worries bring us close to you.

Even if those on the Earth Plane let you down, please believe that those in the Spirit World are always with you, to heal and comfort. We do so, knowing that you may not be aware of us or acknowledge our help, as we are selfless you see, and do not seek validation as those in the earth plane do.

The next time you feel yourself at the edge of the darkness, call upon us, to sit with you.

Sitting with Spirit means you are never alone. You are loved by all whom you have never met and those you have loved. Sit with Spirit, for we are always there to love, heal, and guide

Be the Light

Do not let other people's darkness shadow your light. Do not wait for someone to brighten your day. Be the light for someone else's day by putting a smile on their otherwise worried face or bringing a moment of lightness to their heavy mind.

Let your inner light shine on others, and it will also shine back on you. Giving opens up your heart and mind to receiving good. There will be times when you want to give up and don't feel you have anything to give.

It is easy to fall into a negative space and forget that life can be good and love is out there. By being the light for others and bringing joy to others, we will eventually feel better within ourselves.

So be the light for others, and you, too, will be filled with light

Be Yourself. This is You. This is YOUR life

Stay true to your values and ideals. Don't let society or peer pressure decide or shape a reality that doesn't fit your soul. A lot of us struggle with expectations put on us, so much so that we end up trying to be something we are not. I remember when I first stepped into the "spiritual industry,"

Other mediums told me I didn't look very spiritual or "medium-like." I stood out because there aren't that many Indian mediums, especially one with an accent in the UK. I would opt for a smart casual look—a jacket, jeans, and a top. I didn't have incense, crystals, or a large angel or Buddha on my table during psychic fairs.

When I started, all I had was a tablecloth and my cards. I would see people lining up to get a reading from people with two banners citing "as seen on psychic TV" or "International celebrity psychic" and so on. Most were older and wore flowing dresses; some would adopt a more eccentric look, while I looked too plain and uninteresting.

I would see all this and feel like I wasn't doing enough, that I needed to copy some of what I saw at these fairs. Then my husband, the all-knowing nonspiritual oracle, said to me, "But that is not you at all, Angela. Just be yourself; people will come to you because of you, not what you wear or have on your table," he said wisely.

So, I did me. I did have a banner, but it stated what I offered. It was practical and informative. I did have some crystals, but they were small and sometimes helped keep the flyers in place. I wore more colourful clothes but wore what I felt comfortable in.

Sometimes, our environment will make us think we need to do or be something other than we are. Use these moments to decide what to take and what to leave behind. YOU determine what values, morals, ideals, or external representation you want to show the world. Let it help you understand your meaning. Who are you, and what do you want?

You determine yourself. No one else.

Joyful Spirit

Do not feel threatened by us or call us names given by those who lack the understanding of who we are and of the afterlife.

You only fear what you don't know and this is true of those who spread misinformation and terror of the Spirit World. Our world is different from yours but also familiar because there are many of us here, who have touched the Earth Plane. We have experienced your world and understand your worries, pain, and difficulties. We too, have experienced them during our lives before becoming Spirit.

We also understand your fears of US and of dying. We would like to reassure all of you that we only come in pure love and that death is only of your physical life.

Your Spirit continues to thrive and evolve. We are not ghosts, evil, paranormal, or beings that cause harm. We are, in fact, "Joyful Spirit" because we are full of love and compassion and free from earthly concerns.

We have found true peace in our lives and realised that love is the energy that powers every living being. Spirit has learned, evolved, and lct go of the physical constraints.

We are no longer angry, unhappy, frustrated, purposeless, or in pain. There is only love, and that is all we need. We come to you, dear ones, to share our love and joy with you. So, if we appear to you or make you feel our energy, it is not to harm or scare you; it is to allow us to simply be with each other.

We come to guide you during difficult times and to heal your grief. When your heart yearns for us, it sends us an energetic wave that draws us close. Trust that we will be right there when it's time for you to leave the Earth Plane.

It makes us sad to see so much misinformation and fear in your world, which prevents communication and connection between our worlds.

Our world is joyful and filled with love. We are, therefore, Joyful Spirit.

Be with Love

Do not feel the need to love everyone. Not everyone is for you. Be with people who make you feel worthy. Remember your self-worth always. Keep your communications open and honest. Do not be led by secrets and lies. Appreciate people who appreciate you. Friendship is a two-way relationship, never give more of you than needed. Do not fear walking away from those who hurt or lie to you. Your purpose in life is to be happy and spread happiness. If you cannot be happy or made to be unhappy then find a way to change things. Be with people who are honest and can smile from their eyes. Be with people who will cry and laugh with you.

Follow the love, not the pain. Stay with love

Some Days

Some days I miss you more than others. Some days it hurts more than I can feel. Some days the sore in my heart makes it hard to breathe. Some days I don't want to go on.

Other days, I close my eyes and think of you. I let the tears fall and roll down my neck. Your face appears like the sunshine after the rain. I see your smile and hear your words. Some days it's like you never left.

Sometimes, I think of you before I go to sleep. You enter my dreams so slowly and softly that I almost miss that you were there. You speak to me like you always did; your voice sounds the same, and the glint in your eyes shines brightly like it always did. When I wake up, I only feel the emptiness.

Some days, I wish you never left.

I have learned to keep you close to my heart so that some days are better than others. I listen closely to your voice in my mind and accept the signs you send me.

Some days are better than others and every day brings me closer to you.

Walking Away is an Option

Please know that when you feel out of sorts with people or your spiritual path, walking away is an option. Spirit walks with you to help guide your path, but we do not control it as it will interfere with your free will.

Whenever your heart and mind battle, that is your sign to take a step back and review the situation. Do not let people mistreat you in the name of spirituality or kindness.

Standing up for yourself will not limit your spiritual advancement. It will expand better with accountability and speaking up. We, as Spirit, cannot intervene; however, we help through physical signs in the human body that indicate something is not right, and we touch you through feelings.

When your feelings about a person or situation change, and you want to question what you are told, please take it as a sign from US.

How you deal with it will affect your progress. Every situation offers two options – diplomacy and the other, conflict. It is yours to decide and deal with.

Please remember that situations will arise to help, not hinder, your progress. However, the path you choose will be important. Do not stay in circumstances that compromise your self-worth and happiness.

You are worthy of moving forward and finding the joy of living on the Earth Plane.

Power

There are those amongst you who yearn for power in all aspects of their lives. If used correctly, power can bring positive change and inspire and empower others.

Leaders whose sole purpose is to attain a position of authority to suppress or control others work in the darkness of humanity.

Power is not harmful; the Great Divine bestowed it upon us to help shape society and provide structure. As with many gifts given to Mankind, it has been misused from the beginning of time, and it brings great sadness within the Spirit World to see suffering because of it. At some point, the power-hungry will find success, a short-lived one, or there will be a price to pay.

Looking back, do you know of powerful men surrounded by unfaithful servants who loathe them to the point of murder? Or those who will say untruths to make the influential feel their loyalty? False followers will boost your self-esteem for a while, but they will betray you at some point. Surround yourself with love and kindness, and your power will attract people who will want to support you for your light.

You have a choice about how you create your success and what you do with power. This could relate to relationships, work, friendships, or an organisation. If you choose to do good, then your success will come naturally, and there will be opportunities to inspire while you lead.

On Spirituality as a Religion

The word religion has been tainted by centuries of misconduct and so much so many on the Earth Plane seek less control and more personal freedom in their beliefs. We do acknowledge the need for some form of guidelines, to encourage those who are at the forefront of the religion to continue to do their good work. Sadly, we have seen those who use religion like all others, to inflate their ego and misuse their authority. Spirituality, dear ones, is not a game to play for the fun of it and drop when you are bored. If you are called to serve then do it for the love of Mankind and to improve your Spirituality. Spirituality does not need to be a religion but more of a personal calling to be connected to self and with others who feel the same way. We in Spirit would prefer to call it the collective, rather than religion. Spirituality is the connectivity of consciousness that we in the Spirit world try to encourage. Have you not noticed that like attracts like, and this is the reason many of you gather in Spiritualist Churches and other opportunities such as healing, sound, meditation, and expanding knowledge in the different aspects of self-development? This is done willingly, without the threat of retribution. Spirituality is fluid and has no barriers. Many paths lead to the same place, and your Guides are always there to help you get there. Put your ego aside, and serve if you must, but live a spiritual life first without fuss. Spirituality is not a badge to put on your sleeve but a soothing balm on broken hearts and souls.

The Soulful Robin

I saw a beautiful robin in my garden today,

Just as I thought about you, dear mother,

Was it you, using the robin to show me a sign?

Or was it the butterfly that flew to the rose bush you loved?

The robin sat on the fence, tilted its head to look at me,

Or was it on the piece of cake I had on the table?

Its dark eyes, brightened by the sun, were playful and mysterious. The light summer breeze went through its tiny body, and the magic was broken as he flew off.

I sat and thought about you, dear Robin,

You left me with more questions than answers,

Why did you look at me? Were you my mother in bird form? Are you used by Spirit to show us signs?

Soulful Robin, I don't care why or how,

But seeing you when I was at my lowest brought me peace. I felt my mother in your beautiful eyes, and the comfort you brought to my broken heart is priceless.

Fly-free, always soulful, Robin. You are a blessing to our world, and may you always be our sign from Spirit.

Be Within Your Light

Be within your light, even if it feels like a flicker

Be within your love even if you don't feel loved

Be within your power even if people try to take it away

Be within your heart, even if it's broken

Life will always throw challenges at you, sometimes making you feel powerless. You may even feel something has been taken away from you. These are trying times, and many will fall into depression.

Whatever you experience is temporary, but what must remain within your consciousness is that self-belief.

Honour yourself regardless of the situation, and stay in your power. No one can take it away from you unless you let them.

Just remember that you are enough even if life has broken you. Find a way to patch yourself up like a broken vase.

You are worthy to try, so don't give up.

About the author:

Angela Mitchell was born in Malaysia to second-generation Indian parents before moving to Stockholm, Sweden.

Angela is a spiritual medium, spirit artist, and teacher based in Berkshire but working internationally. She finally embraced her spirituality in 2013 after fighting it since the age of nine. She spent many years in the corporate world, starting with journalism in the 90s and then working as a marketing and events professional in NGOs, government, education, and IT. She is also an artist, and many of her paintings are displayed in homes worldwide.

She comes from a very spiritual family with healers, mediums, and psychics, starting with her Maternal grandmother and aunt. Her parents introduced her to yoga, meditation, and Kundalini awakening from a young age.

Please join Angela's community for free if you would like to connect, learn, and share your spiritual experiences:

Facebook:
https://www.facebook.com/angelamitchellmedium

Angela Mitchell's Spiritual Circle:

https://www.facebook.com/groups/angelamitchellcircle

Website: www.angela-mitchell.co.uk

Printed in Great Britain
by Amazon

49795053R00050